IN THE WORDS OF NAPOLEON
A Collection of Quotations of Napoleon Bonaparte

Drawing by Lawrence J. Savoie
from Brudhon's portrait of Napoleon
painted just prior to Waterloo

IN THE WORDS
OF
NAPOLEON

A Collection of Quotations of Napoleon Bonaparte

Translated and Compiled

by

Daniel Savage Gray

TROY STATE UNIVERSITY PRESS

TROY, ALABAMA 36081

International Standard Book Number: 0-916624-07-2

Library of Congress Catalog Number: 77-071468

To Linda
    -for being

TABLE OF CONTENTS

PREFACE

Napoleon Bonaparte is one of the most fascinating men in history. His personality, loves, and amazing career have piqued the curiosity of scholars and the imagination of romantics. It follows, therefore, that his opinions, judgments, and witticisms would capture the interest of a great number of people. Napoleon was never reluctant to express his opinion on any subject, and more often than not it was an informed opinion. He was a product of the military school system of the Ancien Régime and thus had a sound basic education in the classics, history, mathematics, geometry, and geography. In addition, he loved to read in these subjects and accumulated an impressive traveling library he took on all his campaigns.

Napoleon did not speak in aphorisms. However, after extensive research into the memoirs, diaries, and correspondence of those who knew him, one might think he had. It is in this style that his contemporaries record his opinions and observations. Napoleon's correspondence also reveals many such arresting statements — primarily because he dictated his more than 40,000 letters and orders in a conversational tone, thus giving these passages the impact and immediacy of face-to-face exchanges and often charging them with the knowing skill of a man who expected his words to be remembered and quoted. The aphorisms of Napoleon, which appear with frequency in his own writings or as recorded in those of his friends, enemies, servants, family, or curious by-standers, usually have a tone and substance that make them worthy of remembering. Even Antoine Thibaudeau, an ex-revolutionary and reluctant admirer of Napoleon, conceded that "there was originality and depth in his slightest word."

The purpose of this study is to provide in a single volume and in an interesting format some of Napoleon's remarkable insights into life, love, religion, politics, war, women, and hundreds of other aspects of the human condition. My purpose is to provide a lexicon of opinions and aphorisms of Napoleon. No collection of this kind has ever been produced in English. The only work of similar intent, though totally different in format, is Jules Bertaut's *Napoléon Bonaparte: Virilités; Maximes et Penseés* published in 1912. Every other work which purports to be a collection of the thoughts and opinions of Napoleon includes scores of very lengthy passages which are placed there to instruct the reader as to the mental state, personality, or beliefs of Napoleon. The best of these studies is *The Mind of Napoleon* published in 1955 by J. Christopher Herold. True, a perusal of the quotations I have collected and translated will definitely provide an insight into the character of Napoleon, but this is a happy by-product to my main purpose which is to provide in English translation observations on man and the world that are original, thoughful, and oft-times prophetic — and more remarkable for being uttered by Napoleon.

To answer a question that might trouble many readers — "Did Napoleon really say all these things?" Frankly, nobody can be sure since after his fall from power dozens of anti-Bonapartist memoirs were published by foes and former friends in which numerous unflattering utterances were attributed to him. Then after 1840 and the return of his body to Paris for a hero's interment at L'Invalides, a flood of pro-Napoleon literature appeared with wise and warm opinions attributed to him. The sources upon which the most faith of accuracy may be placed are Napoleon's own letters: the 32 volumes of the *Correspondance de Napoléon Ier Publiée par ordre de l'Empereur Napoléon III* (1858-1870); *Confidential Correspondence of Napoleon Bonaparte with his Brother Joseph, Sometime King of Spain* (1855); *The Unpublished Correspondence of Napoleon I Preserved in the War Archives* (1913); *Lettres inédites de Napoléon Ier* (1897); and *Napoleon, Manuscrits inédites, 1786-1791* (1910). Next in degree of accuracy are the memoirs of those contemporaries who were neither maniacally Bonapartist nor violently anti-Bonapartist: Pierre Roederer's *Autour de Bonaparte* (1909); Francois Mollien's *Mémoires d'un ministre du Trésor public* (1898); Paul de Segur's *Napoléon et la Grande Armée en 1812* (1824); Armand A.L. de Caulaincourt's two volume *Mémoires* (1935-6); and Louis Francois de Baussett's *Mémoires anecdotiques sur l'intérieur du Palais* (1827).

Napoleon as an exile after 1814 fascinated his contemporaries and stimulated the publication of scores of diaries, memoirs, and letters of those who spoke to him and heard him speak in captivity. The best source for quotations during the Elba exile is *Napoleon at Fontainebleau and Elba* (1869) by Sir Neil Campbell, the British commissioner who gradually fell under the sway of Napoleon's personality, but who always maintained an admirable objectivity. The anecdotal fruits of the exile on St. Helena are very abundant, but of quite uneven quality. From the most trustworthy to the highly doubtful are ranged: Gaspard Gourgaud's *Journal de Sainte-Hélène* (1944-7); Henri Bertrand's *Cahiers de Sainte-Hélène* (1951); Tristan de Montholon's *Récits de la captivite de l'Empereur Napoléon* (1847); Emmanuel de Las Cases' *Le Mémorial de Sainte-Hélène* (1822); Barry O'Meara's *Napoleon in Exile, or, A Voice from St. Helena* (1820); and Francesco Antommarchi's *Mémoires du docteur F. Antommarchi* (1825).

Basically pro-Napoleon but nevertheless trustworthy are the recollections of numerous faithful servants and secretaries: Claude Francois de Meneval's *Memoirs of Napoleon Bonaparte* (1910); Francois Fain's *Manuscrit de Mil huit cent treize* (1829); Louis Marchand's *Précis des guerres de César, par Napoléon, écrit par M. Marchand* (1836); Alfred Marquiset's *Napoléon sténographié au conseil d'Etat* (1913); and Louis Etienne St. Denis' *Napoleon; From the Tuileries to St. Helena* (1922).

Less faith should be placed in the statements found in the works of the following individuals who published their memoirs in France during the Bourbon Restoration:

Madame de Remusat's *Memoirs* (1818); Louis A. F. de Bourrienne's *Memoirs of Napoleon Bonaparte* (1828-30); Jean A. C. de Chaptal's *Mes Souvenirs sur Napoléon* (1817); and Constant (Wairy), *Memoirs* (1824). All these suffer for having been written, sometimes by ghost writers, for a Bourbon audience.

The most valuable and accurate secondary sources for this study are the various compilations of Napoleon's words, the best being: Damas Hinard's *Napoléon; ses Opinions et Jugements* (1838); R. M. Johnson's *The Corsican, A Diary of Napoleon's Life in His Own Words* (1930); J. M. Thompson's *Napoleon Self-Revealed* (1934); J. Christopher Herold's *The Mind of Napoleon* (1955); Albert Carr's *Napoleon Speaks* (1941); Maurice Hutt's *Great Lives Observed: Napoleon* (1972); and Conrad Lanza's *Napoleon and Modern War; His Military Maxims* (1954).

Many readers may wonder why the two best-known quotations of Napoleon do not appear — "An army travels on its stomach" and "It is but a step from the sublime to the ridiculous." They are not included for Napoleon never said the first one, and for the second he was merely quoting from the classics. Some readers may raise a final question: "Where, when, and under what circumstances did Napoleon say this?" For the diligent investigator I have given the source of each quotation, but for most readers it is enough that the statement is thought-provoking and that Napoleon Bonaparte — whether the gaunt youth of Arcola and Egypt, or the stern, stout figure of Moscow and Waterloo — said it.

DANIEL SAVAGE GRAY

IN THE WORDS
OF
NAPOLEON

A Collection of Quotations of Napoleon Bonaparte

ADOPTION to AVARICE

ADOPTION

Adoption is an imitation of nature. A child is born naked and without possessions, and so must he come in this condition to the new family which has adopted him.

— Damas Hinard, I, 19

ADULTERY

Adultery is nothing extraordinary — an affair on a couch, a very common occurrence.

— Damas Hinard, I, 28

Adultery on the husband's part should not be sufficient ground for divorce, unless there is the additional circumstance of the husband's keeping his concubine under the same roof as his wife.

— Herold, 23

If a man is unfaithful to his wife, confesses, repents, the affair will be forgotten. The wife gets angry, pardons or makes up and sometimes even comes out ahead. This does not work in reverse, however, if the wife is unfaithful. Even if she confesses and repents, who guarantees that the incident will be forgotten? The wrong cannot be repaired; as a result, she must not, she cannot admit her guilt.

— Damas Hinard, I, 478

ADVISORS

No one can be a good advisor until his career is behind him.

— Martel, III, 5

ALLIES

There is nothing like having friends in time of war. One does not need many of them . . . . They take the place of so much else.

— Bertrand, I, 119

It is better to have an open enemy than a doubtful ally.
— *Table Talk,* 37

AMBASSADORS

Ambassadors are, in the full sense of the term, titled spies.

— *Correspondance de Napoléon,*
No. 8852, X, 606

AMBITION

Ambition achieves what self-interest has begun.
— Caulaincourt, I, 306

The ambition to dominate minds is the strongest of all the passions.

— Bertaut, 42

Ambition and comforts do not go together.
— Bertrand, II, 231

Ambition is what principally motivates men.
— Chaptal, 324

Ambition leads all men. Men of letters as well as others.
— Bertrand, II, 227

Ambition . . . is like all excessive passions — a violent, thoughtless fever that ceases only when life ceases.

— Masson and Biagi, 573

AMERICANS

The Americans are only merchants who put all their glory into making money.

— Gourgaud, II, 316

ANARCHY

Anarchy always leads back to an absolute government.

— Bertaut, 76

ARISTOCRACY

The essence of aristocracy is never to change.

— Bertrand, I, 183

It is the true, sole support of a monarchy — its moderator, its lever, its strong point. A state without it is a rudderless ship, a balloon in the air.

— Las Cases, II, 42

An order of nobility is bearable in a military country; in a commercial one it is intolerable.

— Thompson, 172

Aristocracy always exists. Destroy it in the nobility, it at once removes itself to the rich and powerful houses of the middle class. Destroy it there, it survives and takes refuge with the leaders of the workshops and with the people.

— Damas Hinard, I, 84

In England, everything revolves around the upper classes. Everything is done by and for them. In France, everything is done for the sake of the people.

— Bertrand, I, 63

Nothing is more cowardly than an aristocracy that is afraid; nothing more terrible than when it has nothing to fear.

— Bertrand, I, 93

ARMY

A perfect army would be one in which each officer knew what to do according to circumstances; the best army is that which comes closest to this.

— Gourgaud, II, 425

The strength of an army, like power in mechanics, is the product of the mass by the velocity.

— Lanza, 15

ASSASSINATION

There are different ways of assassinating a man: the pistol, the sword, poison, or morally assassinating . . . . It is the same in the end, excepting that the latter is the most cruel.

— O'Meara, II, 139

ASTRONOMY

It's a splendid amusment, and a superb branch of science.

— Johnston, 9

Among all the sciences astronomy is the one which has rendered the greatest services to reason and to commerce.

— Johnston, 51

To share the night between a beautiful woman and a lovely sky; to spend the day checking observation by calculation — that is happiness on earth.

— Johnston, 51

ATHEISM

To fear death is to profess atheism.

— Bertaut, 159

The atheist is a better subject than the fanatic: the one obeys, the other kills.

— Bertaut, 158

Wishing to be an atheist does not make you one.

— Antommarchi, II, 118

AVARICE

One who worships the golden calf may have money, but not honor.

— Ludwig, 554

Avarice has its inconveniences, but to a lesser degree than poverty.

— Bertrand, I, 209

B
BATTLE to BUREAUCRATS

BATTLE

A battle is a dramatic action which has a beginning, a middle, and an end. The order of battle which the two armies take, the first movements to come to blows – this is the exposition; the counter-movements of the army under attack form the complication, which requires new dispositions and brings on the crisis from which springs the result or dénouement.

– Damas Hinard, I, 131

A battle sometimes decides everything; and sometimes the most trifling thing decides the fate of a battle.

– O'Meara, I, 128

The fate of a battle is the result of a single instant – a thought . . . . The decisive moment comes, a moral spark is lighted, and the smallest reserve accomplishes victory.

– Bertaut, 184

BAYONET

For the brave, a musket is only the handle for a bayonet.

– Bertaut, 180

It is the bayonet which has always been the weapon of the brave and the principal instrument of victory.

– *Correspondance de Napoléon,*
No. 1311, II, 250-1

I had sooner see a soldier without his breeches than without his bayonet.

– Johnston, 52

6

BEAUTY

Only that which is large is beautiful.

— Bertaut, 44

Enticement reaches the heart through the eyes. One is always tempted to yield to that which one admires.

— Bertaut, 46

BUDGET

The great art is to do in every year no more than is requisite.

— *Correspondence of Napoleon with Joseph,* No. 365, I, 303

With budgets one could create the world.

— Johnston, 483

BUREAUCRATS

Timid and cowardly soldiers are the reason why nations lose their independence; but pusillanimous officials destroy the majesty of the law, the rights of the throne, and social order itself.

— Hutt, 44

CAPITALISM

Whilst an individual owner, with a personal interest in his property, is always wide awake, and brings his plans to fruition, communal interest is inherently sleepy and unproductive; because individual enterprise is a matter of instinct, and communal enterprise a matter of public spirit — and that is rare.

— Thompson, 66

CELIBACY

It was one of the means whereby the Court of Rome attempted to rivet the chains of Europe by preventing the cleric from being a citizen.

— Johnston, 228

CENSORSHIP

Controlled by the government, a free press may become a strong ally . . . . To leave it to its own devices is to sleep beside a powder keg.

— Montholon, II, 88

Whenever news arrives which is disagreeable to the government, its publication must be delayed until people are so sure of the truth that it no longer needs to be said because everybody knows it.

— Holtman, 164-5

The printing press is an arsenal; it cannot be common property.

— Bertaut, 78

It would be impossible to have a free press in France; the government would not last a day.

> — Bertrand, I, 71

Ideas are the worst enemies of kings.

> — Damas Hinard, I, 118

Newspapers should be limited to advertising.

> — Bertaut, 78

I do not want censorship ... because I do not wish to be held responsible for all the drivel which appears in print.

> — Carr, 215

CHANCE

Accident, hazard, chance, whatever you choose to call it, a mystery to ordinary minds, becomes a reality to superior men.

> — Rémusat, 135

CHARACTER

Men are what we make them, and their characters improve according to the way we treat them.

> — Bertrand, I, 247

The true character of a person always reveals itself in critical circumstances ... and there are some sleepers whose awakening is terrifying.

> — Damas Hinard, I, 199

A man is known by his conduct to his wife, to his family, and to those under him.

> — O'Meara, I, 287

The private life of a man is a mirror where one can read and be fruitfully educated.

— Bertaut, 40

To really understand a man, we must judge him in misfortune.

— *Table Talk,* 149

CHEMISTRY

Chemistry has . . . made such progress, that it is possible it may effect a revolution in commercial relations as extraordinary as that caused by the discovery of the compass.

— Miot de Melito, 573

CHILDREN

There is no beating about the bush with them. They say naturally whatever comes into their heads. If they are greedy, they ask without hesitation. Ah! the little belly always rules.

— St. Denis, 240-1

CHRISTIANITY

If this is not the true religion, one is very excusable in being deceived, for everything in it is grand and worthy of God.

— *Table Talk,* 116

The Christian religion is that of a highly civilized people. It elevates man; it proclaims the superiority of spirit over matter and of the soul over the body.

— *Correspondance de Napoléon,*
  "Affaires religieuses," XXIX, 568

The Christian religion is all Greek and of the school of Plato.

— Bertrand, II, 341

This religion does not excite courage. There is too much horror of unexpected death. It takes too much care to go to heaven.

— Bertrand, I, 120

Can you conceive of a dead man making conquests with an army faithful and entirely devoted to his memory? ... Can you conceive of Caesar, ... from the depths of his mausoleum governing the empire, watching over the destinies of Rome? Such is the history of the invasion and conquest of the world by Christianity. Such is the power of the God of the Christians.

— *Table Talk,* 118

CIVIL WAR

When once the torches of civil war are lighted, the military leaders are only the means of victory; it is the crowd who rules.

— Bertaut, 175

CLEMENCY

Clemency, properly speaking, is such a poor little virtue when it is not founded on policy.

— Rémusat, 102-3

CLERGY

The clergy is a power that never is quiet. Against you unless it is for you, it serves none free of charge. You cannot be under obligations to it, wherefore you must be its master.

— Caulaincourt, I, 392

The teachers of religion . . . are eternally preaching up that their kingdom is not of this world, and yet seize everything which they can lay their hands upon.

— O'Meara, I, 273

People judge the power of God by the power of priests.

— Bertaut, 157

The priests are no longer to be feared in our time; they lost all their power on the day when their supremacy in science passed to the layman.

— Johnston, 162

CLOTHES

Women's clothes are a quite ruinous expense, and a very bad investment.

— Bertrand, I, 69

What matter what your wife wears? If you are alone she won't dress up for you. Therefore, she only dresses for others, which is sheer coquetry or a matter of pride.

— Bertrand, I, 69

COLONIES

All the colonies will follow the example of the United States. You grow tired of waiting for orders from five thousand miles away; tired of obeying a government which seems foreign to you because it is remote, and because of necessity it subordinates you to its own local interest, which it cannot sacrifice to yours.

— Caulaincourt, I, 305

One must govern colonies with force, but never force without justice.

— Bertaut, 146

12

As soon as colonies feel strong enough to resist, they want to shake off the yoke of those who created them. One's country is where one lives; a man does not take long to forget that he or his father was born under another sky.

— Caulaincourt, I, 305-6

CONCEIT

The greatest happiness that could befall him would be if he could persuade everyone that his grandfather had come out of the Ark.

— Caulaincourt, I, 344

CONCEPTION

The man takes much more of a part in propagation than the woman. She is like the soil which produces all kinds of fruit: some wheat, some trees. The male impregnates, determines the sex, and has the most realistic part in the kind and question of the children.

— Bertrand, II, 228

CONFIDENCE

Fear and uncertainty accelerate the fall of empires: they are a thousand times more fatal than the dangers and losses of an ill-fated war.

— *Correspondance de Napoléon,*
No. 8237, X, 116

Commerce exists only through confidence. There is no confidence under a weak government. There is no confidence in a country where there are factions.

— Bertaut, 132

Confidence cannot be commanded.

— O'Meara, II, 162

CONGRESS

A [diplomatic] congress is a fiction agreed upon by the diplomats. It is the pen of Machiavelli united with the sword of Mohammed.

— Bertaut, 29

CONQUEST

There is no doubt that conquest is a combination of war and politics.

— Bertrand, II, 216

A conquerer must not inspire a good opinion of his benevolence until he has demonstrated that he can be severe with malefactors.

— Carr, 248

CONSCRIPTION

Conscription is, for the family, the most dreaded and detestable law; but it maintains the security of the state.

—Damas Hinard, I, 275

Without the conscription there can be neither power nor national independence.

— Constant, II, 42

CONSPIRACY

When it comes to conspiracy, everything is permissible.

— Johnston, 108

CONSTITUTION

A constitution should be short — and obscure.

— Johnston, 115

Constitutions are the work of time, and it is impossible to leave too much leeway for improvements.

— Damas Hinard, I, 287

CONVICTION

Force is always force, enthusiasm is only enthusiasm; but conviction remains and engraves itself on the heart.

— Bertaut, 39

CORRUPTION

The exposure of a dishonest accountant is a victory for the government.

— Thompson, 123

A new set of mayors, assessors, or municipal councillors has generally meant nothing more than a fresh form of robbery.

— Thompson, 67

CORSICAN

A Corsican never misses a shot.

— Bertrand, II, 340

COUNCIL

A council of war always makes the worst choice — in war, the most pusillanimous.

— Bertaut, 175

COUP D'ETAT

Where the government is weak, the army rules. A corporal could take over such a government in a moment of crisis.

— Damas Hinard, I, 494

COURAGE

Courage is not counterfeit. It is one virtue untouched by hypocrisy.

— Bertaut, 181

True heroism consists of being superior to the ills of life, in whatever shape they may challenge [one] to the combat.

— Warden, 58

Bravery is an innate quality; one cannot acquire it. It is in the blood. Courage comes from thought: bravery is often only impatience with danger.

— Bertaut, 183

The man who lacks courage is not French.

— Damas Hinard, I, 322

One is only brave for others.

— Bertaut, 184

Courage is like love — it needs hope for nourishment.

— Bertaut, 177

COWARDICE

To avoid one's own danger by making the situation more dangerous for others is clearly cowardice.

— Heinl, 317

CREDIT

Credit is the ruin of agricultural nations, the life-blood of manufacturing nations.

— Bertaut, 135

CREMATION

It is the best mode as then the corpse does not produce any inconvenience; and as to the resurrection, . . .it is easy to the Being who has it in his power to perform such a miracle as bringing the remains of bodies together, also to form again the ashes of the dead.

— O'Meara, I, 171

CRIME

If crimes and misdemeanors increase, that is proof that misery is increasing and that society is poorly governed. Their decrease is proof of the contrary.

— Montholon, II, 88

Many men are criminals only because of their weakness for the ladies.

—Bertaut, 59

CRITICS

[Literary] journals now never criticize with the intention of repressing mediocrity, guiding inexperience, or encouraging rising merit. All their endeavour is to wither, to destroy.

— *Table Talk,* 29

CRUELTY

Great men are never cruel except from necessity.

— Rémusat, 103

CROMWELL

Cromwell ruled for four years. He won only two battles. Cromwell and I have nothing in common.

— Bertrand, I, 8

CULTURE

The French people set a higher value upon the acquisition of a learned mathematician, a famous painter, or a distinguished exponent of any branch of study, than upon that of the richest and most populous city in the world.

— Thompson, 27

D

DEATH to DRUM

DEATH

Death is nothing; but to live defeated and without glory is to die every day.

> — *Correspondance de Napoléon,*
> No. 8209, X, 86

Death may expiate faults, but it does not repair them.

> — *Table Talk,* 149

Death overtakes the coward, but never the brave man till his hour is come.

> — *Table Talk,* 149

Death is nothing but a sleep without dreams.

> — Constant, I, 162

DEBASEMENT

Whatever debases man cannot be serviceable.

> — O'Meara, I, 124

DEBT

One should cultivate one's taste in proportion to one's income.

> — Bertrand, I, 68

The system of continual borrowing, which continually links the present with the past, does in some degree compel confidence in the future.

> — Caulaincourt, I, 300

The first, and most important thing for happiness is never to incur any debts. The second is to spend no more than two-thirds of one's income.

— Bertrand, I, 68

DECEPTION

Nothing betrays weakness more than the attempt to deceive.

— Ludwig, 587

It is easier to deceive than to undeceive.

— Bertaut, 28

Dissimulation, which comes naturally at a maturer age, has to be practiced and learned in youth.

— Carr, 250

DECORATIONS

A soldier will fight long and hard for a bit of colored ribbon.

— Heinl, 22

It is with baubles that men are led.

— Bertaut, 44

DEMOCRACY

A reasonable democracy limits itself just to allowing to everyone an equal chance to compete and obtain.

— Las Cases, II, 43

Democracy may run mad, but it has a heart, it can be moved; an aristocracy always remains cold, and never forgives.

— Johnston, 488

Democracy establishes sovereignty; aristocracy alone preserves it.

> — Las Cases, I, 499

DEPRESSION

The thoughts of the night are not gay.

> — Bertrand, I, 118

DETERMINATION

Impossible? That word is not French.

> — *Table Talk,* 10

DIPLOMACY

The first quality of a diplomat is the ability to keep silent.

> — *Correspondance de Napoléon,*
> No. 6165, VII, 648

In the dealings of one great nation with another, facts say more than words, and public opinion holds the helm.

> — Thompson, 288

In order to demand peace, we need money, steel, and soldiers.

> — *Moniteur,* March 5, 1800

It is always advisable to negotiate. It gives one a means of learning what is going on, and it slows down any preparations for war.

> — Bertrand, I, 66

To talk is not to negotiate.

> — Bertrand, II, 345

DISCIPLINE

If you make everything difficult, the really hard things seem less so.

— Caulaincourt, I, 175

A good general, a good staff, good organization, good instruction, and good and severe discipline make good troops regardless of the cause for which they fight.

— Damas Hinard, II, 542

If there were a single privilege granted to anyone, no matter whom, not one man would obey the order to march.

— Caulaincourt, I, 367

DIVORCE

It would be a great misfortune if it became a national habit.

— Johnston, 152

There are only three valid grounds for divorce: attempted murder, adultery, and impotence.

— Ludwig, 167

DOCTORS

A doctor would rather die than not try to persuade a dying man that he is not ill!

— Johnston, 504

You medical people will have more lives to answer for in the other world than even we generals.

— O'Meara, II, 144

A physician appears ... to resemble a general officer. He must be a man of observation and discernment, with a penetrating eye. Possessed of these qualities, he will discover the strength of the enemy's position. A sagacious practitioner will just employ sufficient force to dispossess the enemy of his stronghold: a force beyond that might injure the citadel.

— Warden, 189

When a man has not confidence in his physician it is useless to have one.

— O'Meara, II, 162

DRAMA

Great tragic drama is the school of great men ... Tragedy excites the soul, lifts the heart, can and ought to create heroes.

— Las Cases, I, 401

Politics must replace on our stage the fatality of the ancients ... The principle of political necessity is a rich source of strong emotions, a fertile germ of the most dramatic situations, a new fate no less imperious, no less ineluctable than that of the ancients.

— Herold, 149

DRUM

The drum imitates the noise of the cannon; it is the best of all instruments — and, it is never out of tune.

— Damas Hinard, II, 523

E
EAST to EXPERIENCE

EAST

Europe is a mole-hill. There have never been great empires and revolutions except in the East, where there are 600,000,000 men.

— Bourrienne, I, 131

ECONOMISTS

They are mere visionaries, who are dreaming of plans of finance while they are unfit to fulfil the duties of a schoolmaster in the most insignificant village.

— Bourrienne, III, 171

If there existed a monarchy of granite, the abstractions of economists would suffice to reduce it to dust.

— Las Cases, I, 755

EDUCATION

The true conquests, the only ones that do not cause regret, are those that are won over ignorance.

— *Correspondance de Napoléon,*
No. 2392, III, 614

It is dangerous for people who are not rich to gain too extensive a knowledge of mathematics.

— *Correspondance de Napoléon,*
No. 8472, X, 320

Something is surely lacking in a great state if a young student cannot get competent advice on the subject he wishes to study, and is obliged to grope his way, wasting months or years in fruitless reading, whilst he searches for the information he really needs.

— Thompson, 185

Of all our institutions, public education is the most important. Everything depends on it, the present and the future.

— Molé, I, 61

The doctorate should not be granted too easily . . . It is not necessary that everybody becomes a *docteur*.

— Damas Hinard, II, 552

EMOTIONS

Most sentiments are traditions. We feel them because they have preceded us.

— Las Cases, I, 271

Every emotion debases except hatred.

— Damas Hinard, I, 557

Angry people never maintain that they are angry, and . . . those who are frightened say they have no fear.

— Abbott, 116

If we do not see things through our passions, we see them through our interests.

— Rémusat, 83

An honorable man always attempts to control his feelings.

— Hortense, II, 357

ENGLAND

There are only two nations, France and England; all the rest are nothing.

— Rémusat, 584

England is said to traffic in everything. Why then does she not sell liberty, for which she might get a high price, and without any fear of exhausting her stock?

— *Table Talk,* 79

There are more honorable men in England proportionately than in any other country — but then there are some very bad; they are in extremes.

— Malcolm, 103

These English are a ferocious race; what crimes are in their history.

— Rosebery, 197

They have something of the bulldog in them; they love blood.

— Rosebery, 195

EGYPT

It is the geographical key to the world.

— Bertaut, 312

EQUALITY

Equality exists only in theory.

— Bertaut, 24

EVIL

Evil is always individual, nearly never collective. The brothers of Joseph could not resolve to kill him, but Judas, coldly, hypocritically, with craven calculation, delivered over his master for execution.

— Las Cases, I, 271

A philosopher has maintained that men are born evil. It would be a lengthy project — and a pointless one — to explore the truth of his statement.

— Las Cases, I, 271

EVOLUTION

There is a link between animals and the Deity. Man is merely a more perfect animal than the rest. He reasons better . . . Plants are so many animals which eat and drink; and there are gradations up to man, who is only the most perfect of them all. The same spirit animates them all in a greater or a lesser degree.

— O'Meara, I, 123

EXPERIENCE

Nations and individuals alike learn only from their own experience — and, most of the time, from misfortunes.

— Herold, 58

F

FAME to FRANCE

FAME

A great reputation is a great noise. Laws, institutions, monuments, nations, all fall; but the noise continues and resounds in after ages.

— Bourrienne, I, 314

In war men may lose in a day what [fame] they have spent years building up.

— Caulaincourt, I, 305

He who fears to lose his reputation is certain to lose it.

— *Correspondance de Napoléon,*
No. 1735, II, 641

Fame has its beauties, but in recollection and the imagination.

— *Correspondance de Napoléon,*
No. 4674, VI, 241

Better never to have lived than to exist and pass without leaving a trace.

— Ludwig, 567

Human pride finds the public it desires in that ideal world which is called posterity.

— Rémusat, 83

He who believes that a hundred years hence, a fine poem, or even a line in one, will recall a great action of his own, or that a painting will commemorate it, has his imagination fired by that idea. The battlefield has no dangers, the cannon roars in vain; to him it is only that

28

sound which, a thousand years hence, will carry a brave man's name to the ears of our distant descendents.

— Rémusat, 83

Posterity is the only judge of kings; only it has the right to reward or to refuse honors.

— Damas Hinard, II, 327

FANATICISM

Fanaticism is always the child of persecution.

— O'Meara, I, 219

Military fanaticism is the only kind that is good for anything. It is required if men are to let themselves be killed.

— Damas Hinard, I, 471

In the heads of fanatics there are no organs which reason has the power to penetrate.

— Damas Hinard, I, 470

Of all assassins, fanatics are the most dangerous; it is very difficult to protect oneself from the ferocity of these men. A man who has the intention, the will, to sacrifice himself, is always master of the life of another man.

— St. Denis, 244-5

FASTING

Oh what a beast is man, to believe that abstaining from flesh, and eating fish, which is so much more delicate and delicious, constitutes fasting. Poor man.

— O'Meara, I, 295-6

FATALISM

Fatalism is only a word. The Turks themselves, those masters of fatalism, are not convinced of it; otherwise, the art of medicine would no longer exist in their country.

— Damas Hinard, I, 471

FEDERAL GOVERNMENT

The federal system is contrary to the interests of large nations since it fragments authority.

— *Correspondance de Napoléon,*
No. 6483, VII, 164

FINALITY

Everything has its end — beauty, wit, feeling, the sun itself.

— Carr, 252

FLATTERY

Talent likes to be flattered.

— Bertrand, I, 14

He who can flatter can also malign.

— Bertaut, 28

Praise from an enemy is to be suspected. It can flatter a man of honor only when given after the cessation of hostilities.

— Bertaut, 173

FOOL

The fool has a great advantage over an intelligent man — he is always content with himself.

— Bertaut, 41

FORCE

Force is only justifiable in extremes; when we have the upper hand, justice is preferable.

— Heinl, 121

Force is the law of animals; men are governed by conviction.

— Masson and Biagi, 528

FORTUNE

Profit by the favor of fortune when its caprices are for you; fear that it will change to spite. Fortune is a woman.

— Damas Hinard, I, 486

FRANCE

The French nation . . . will as soon do without bread as without glory.

— O'Meara, I, 239

Valour and love of glory are an instinct with the French, a sort of sixth sense.

— *Table Talk,* 68

There is nothing the French will not do at the appearance of danger, it seems to give them spirit, it is their Gallic heritage.

— *Table Talk,* 68

Trifles are great things in France — reason nothing.

— Malcolm, 95

Everybody reasons in France. Flighty and frivolous, yes; but nobody forgets anything here.

— Caulaincourt, II, 192

The French never forgive cowardice.

— Caulaincourt, I, 356

The French are all critical, turbulent: they are real weathervanes at the mercy of the winds.

— Johnston, 473

The French admire only the impossible.

— Bertaut, 193

It is in the French character to exaggerate, to complain, and to distort.

— Damas Hinard, I, 491

The French are like women. You must not stay away from them too long.

— Caulaincourt, I, 203

Oh! They are a fickle people.

— Campbell, 238

Luxury and glory have never failed to turn the heads of the French.

— Rémusat, 434

The French are to be ruled through their vanity.

— Rémusat, 47

Your good Frenchman loves flattery.

— Caulaincourt, I, 376

The French don't like liberty as much as equality. It is especially the nobility they hate.

— Bertrand, I, 183

She is among the nations of Europe what the lion is amongst the other animals.

— Montholon, II, 5

The French are always ready to eat out of one's hand. They lack seriousness; consequently, that quality impresses them most.

— Caulaincourt, I, 338

The besetting sin of the French people is not overwork.

— Thompson, 169

Frenchmen are never happy out of France.

— Thompson, 122

When a Frenchman is caught between fear of the police and fear of the devil, he sides with the devil.

— Roederer, 6

GAMBLING

Gambling is necessary in all societies.

— Bertrand, II, 341

GENERALSHIP

The first quality of a commander-in-chief is a cool head, one that receives correct impressions and is not dazzled or intoxicated by good news or bad.

— Damas Hinard, I, 519

He who cannot look dry-eyed upon a battlefield will allow many men to be killed uselessly.

— Bertaut, 172

The principal talent of a general consists in understanding the mentality of his soldiers and winning their confidence.

— Chaptal, 296

True wisdom in a general means energy.

— Lanza, 88

Better an army of deer commanded by a lion, than an army of lions commanded by a deer.

— Méneval, III, 878

A commander-in-chief must never allow rest to either the victors or the vanquished.

— Bertaut, 171

The glory and honor of his arms is the first object that a general who gives battle must consider; the safety and conservation of his men is only secondary; but in audacity and obstinacy a general finds the safety and conservation of his men.

— Damas Hinard, I, 522

Following maxims does not make a great general. War is a business that is governed by the actual moment.

— Bertrand, I, 5

History has its uses, but it won't make a general.

— Bertrand, I, 5

Read and meditate on the wars of the greatest captains; this is the only means of rightly learning the science of war.

— Montholon, III, 192

Generals must use greater strategy after battles than before, for it is then, when they are forced to make some decisions, that they are criticized by all those who favor other measures.

— Carr, 75

Speeches preceding a battle do not make soldiers brave; the old soldiers scarcely listen, and the recruits forget them at the first cannon shot.

— Lanza, 81

GENIUS

Genius is a flame which comes from heaven, but which rarely finds a head prepared to receive it.

— Bertaut, 47

Genius must exist wherever there is a creation.

— Rémusat, 135

In war, genius is thought in action.

— Bertaut, 180

Genius is the art of combining ideas.

— Chaptal, 324

It is characteristic of genius to show indulgence of others.

— Carr, 24

Every man of genius, every office-holder in the Republic of Letters, in whatever country he may have been born, is a French citizen.

— Thompson, 27

GEOGRAPHY

Its domain grows in like measure with the extension of the human spirit; it is enriched by discoveries; it is subject to change by the effects of revolutions – political and physical.

— *Correspondance de Napoléon*
No. 12416, XV, 132

GOD

There is but one God, the father of victory, who graciously fights on the side of good.

— Ludwig, 120

GOSPELS

The morality of the Gospel is that of equality;

therefore, it is the most favorable to a republican government.

— Bertaut, 154

Very beautiful parables, excellent moral teaching, but very few facts.

— Bertaut, 113

GOVERNMENT

Governments keep their promises only when forced to or when it is to their advantage.

— Gourgaud, I, 481

Not allowing men to grow old in their jobs is the great art of government.

— *Correspondance de Napoléon,*
No. 858, I, 665

Old works will not drive new machines.

— Rémusat, 477

Stability in the personnel makes everything stable.

— Caulaincourt, II, 242

At the center of society, like the sun, is the government. The numerous institutions must revolve around it never wandering from their orbits.

— Mollien, I, 261

What does the art of government consist in, whether for sovereigns or ministers? It consists in advertising anything well done.

— Thompson, 189

The art of government consists not only in punishing the wicked, but also in rewarding the good.

— Thompson, 102

There is nothing absolutely new: political institutions do but revolve in a circle, and it is often necessary to return to what has been done before.

— Miot de Melito, 354

Violent remedies discredit the legislator.

— Thompson, 46

Wherever there is mystery, there are always bad intentions.

— O'Meara, II, 154

The true path of a government is to employ the aristocracy, but with the form and intent of democracy.

— Bertaut, 73-4

It is not fair to judge of the character of a people by the conduct of their government.

— Maitland, 188

Only those who wish to govern for their own advantage and to deceive the masses could wish to keep them in ignorance. The more enlightened the masses are, the more people will be convinced of the necessity of laws and the need to protect them, and the more tranquil, contented, and prosperous society will be.

— Las Cases, I, 271

The only time that the enlightenment of the masses could ever do harm would be if the government, in opposition to the good of the people, forced them to the wall or reduced the lowest classes to misery and starvation — then the more intelligent course of action would be self-defense or crime.

— Las Cases, I, 271

GRATITUDE

Ah, gratitude! That is a poetic word which has no meaning in times of revolution.

— Rémusat, 82

We attach ourselves more easily to those we have benefited than to our benefactors.

— Gourgaud, II, 201

GREAT MEN

A man, to be really great, no matter in what order of greatness, must have actually improvised a portion of his own glory — must have shown himself superior to the event which he has brought about.

— Rémusat, 135

Great men are meteors destined to be consumed in illuminating the earth.

— Bertaut, 27

Is it because they are lucky that they become great men? No, but because they are great they are able to master luck.

— Las Cases, II, 575

It was not the Roman army conquered Gaul, but Caesar; it was not the Carthaginians made the armies of the Republic tremble at the very gates of Rome, but Hannibal; it was not the Macedonian army marched to the Indus, but Alexander.

— Johnston, 143

Great men love the glory of those who resemble them.

— Constant, I, 122

GUERILLA WAR

Such a war, by becoming protracted, demoralizes an army, but steels a nation.

— Thiebault, IV, 110

H

HAPPINESS

A quiet life, spent in the enjoyment of one's own tastes and of the affection of one's family – that . . . is the happiest choice.

– Thompson, 14

Happiness lies in sleep.

– Johnston, 502

HATE

A true man never hates. His anger and ill-humor never last beyond the present moment – [like] electric shocks.

– Las Cases, II, 609

There are men to whom hatred is a necessity . . . they find relief in sowing dissension and discord.

– Carr, 80

HEART

Heart! How the devil do you know what your heart is? It is a bit of you crossed by a big vein in which the blood goes quicker when you run.

– Fisher, 210

The human heart is an abyss which frustrates all calculation. The most penetrating gaze cannot fathom it.

– *Correspondance de Napoléon,*
No. 7598, IX, 348

It is as necessary for the heart to feel as for the body to be fed.

— Table Talk, 150

HEAVEN

Paradise is a central spot whither the souls of men proceed along different roads; every sect has a road of its own.

— Johnston, 145

There are many roads to paradise and upright men have always managed to find their own, from Socrates to the Quakers.

— Marquiset, 29

HELL

God in his infinite mercy could never tolerate such a thing.

— Las Cases, 162

HISTORIAN

The historian must instruct, make the facts and causes known and explain them.

— Bertrand, II, 358

The historian like the orator must persuade; he must convince.

— Bertrand, II, 344

Where there is the marvelous, the historian disappears and the poet appears.

— Bertrand, II, 344

They copy that which their predecessors have written, so that their opinions and interest are not opposed to it, without troubling themselves to inquire into truth or even probabilities.

— *Table Talk,* 148

HISTORY

History paints the human heart.

— *Moniteur,* December 21, 1812

Nations have diseases just like men and their case histories would be as interesting to write as those of human ills.

— Chaptal, 308

This is the only true philosophy.

— Montholon, III, 190

Men should read nothing else.

— Carr, 27

The reading of history is a science in itself. Everything has been said over and over again. There is such a glut of apocryphal histories . . . that a man who wants to look up the best account of some event, and plunges into a big historical library, loses himself in a regular maze.

— Thompson, 183

There is one part of history that cannot be learned from books; it is that epoch that is nearest to our own times.

— *Correspondance de Napoléon,*
No. 12416, XV, 133-4

It is in history that one must look for the advantages and disadvantages of different laws.

— *Moniteur,* December 21, 1812

HOMER

Homer, in his epic, was poet, orator, historian, lawgiver, geographer, and theologian. He was the encyclopedist of his age.

— Damas Hinard, I, 573

Homer must have been to war; all the details of his battles ring true. On every page can be found the very face of war.

— Bertrand, I, 72

HONOR

The tribunal of honor is the foundation-stone of an army. If this be destroyed, discipline and bravery will vanish with it.

— *Table Talk,* 193

A nation can replace men more easily than honor.

— Breed, 178

Honor is the best currency.

— Thompson, 223

Wounded honor does not heal.

— Segur, 34

HUNGER

Hunger — the belly — rules the world.

— Damas Hinard, II, 570

HYPOCHONDRIAC

He is constantly surprised that when he is sick anyone else should be well.

— Hortense, II, 437

I
IDEOLOGY to ITALIANS

IDEOLOGY

Ideology tries to base government on shaky theory instead of on laws which grow from knowledge of the human heart and from the lessons of history.

— *Moniteur,* December 21, 1812

IMAGINATION

Imagination rules the world. By that alone can man be governed; without it he is but a brute.

— Johnston, 140

IMMORALITY

Immorality is, without doubt, the most fatal inclination for the sovereign . . . since he makes it fashionable . . . and it infects society like a disease. It is the scourge of a nation.

— Damas Hinard, I, 585

IMMORTALITY

Immortality is the recollection one leaves in the memory of man.

— Bourrienne, II, 77

A regiment is never destroyed by the enemy; it is immortalized.

— Johnston, 55

IMPOSSIBLE

Impossible is a word the meaning of which is wholly relative; every man has his "impossible" according to his capacity.

— Hutt, 62

The impossible is the spectre of the timid and the refuge of the coward.

— Molé, I, 149

In the mouth of power, the word is a confession of impotence.

— Molé, I, 149

INDECISION

The man who has lost courage is indecisive because every alternative facing him is undesirable.

— Damas Hinard, I, 589

The worst thing in any venture is indecision.

— Damas Hinard, I, 589

INDIVIDUALITY

What a pitiful machine man is, after all! Not one bodily wrapping like another; not one soul that does [not] differ from all the rest.

— Ludwig, 629

A man cannot be extraordinary without being unlike others.

— Johnston, 439

INFANTRY

The infantry is the soul of the army.
— Bertaut, 186

INGRATITUDE

Do you know what pierces the heart most deeply? It is the ingratitude of man.
— *Table Talk,* 48

I deem ingratitude the greatest weakness anyone can have.
— Ludwig, 557

INSANITY

Madness is the last stage of human degradation. It is the abdication of humanity. Better to die a thousand times.
— *Table Talk,* 48

INSINUATION

There is nothing in the world makes a man hate another so much as insinuations; especially when they come from one in power, because he cannot repel or answer them.
— O'Meara, II, 155

INSTITUTIONS

Men are powerless to insure the future; institutions alone fix the fate of nations.
— *Correspondance de Napoléon,*
No. 22023, XXVIII, 300

INSUBORDINATION

Insubordination may only be the evidence of a strong mind.

— Heinl, 217

INTELLECTUALS

Savants and intellectuals are like coquettes. One may see them and talk with them, but do not make one your wife or the other your official.

— *Correspondance de Napoléon,*
No. 12924, XV, 537

A fool is only boring; a pedant is unbearable.

— Bertaut, 103

There are some men capable of translating a poem who are incapable of leading fifteen men.

— *Correspondance de Napoléon,*
No. 9699, XI, 554

Society in the salons is always in a state of hostility against the government. Everything is criticized and nothing praised.

— Caulaincourt, I, 368

INTIMIDATION

A great people may be killed, but they cannot be intimidated.

— Heinl, 204

IRRITATION

This man's disposition makes him like a person afflicted

with an inveterate itch; he has need of continually rubbing against something.

– O'Meara, II, 228

ISLAM

The difference between Christianity and Islam . . . is that the first is a threat – the religion of fear, while the other is a promise – the religion of enticement.

– Damas Hinard, I, 243

The Moslems . . . tore more souls away from false gods, toppled more idols, pulled down more pagan temples in fifteen years than the followers of Moses and Christ had in fifteen centuries.

– Correspondance de Napoléon,
"Affaires religieuses," XXIX, 570

ITALIANS

Divided by as many interests as there are cities, effeminate and corrupt, as big cowards as they are hypocrites, the people of Italy . . . are ill-made for liberty.

– Correspondance de Napoléon,
No. 2318, III, 530-1

A people as soft as they are supersitious, and as cowardly as they are contemptible.

– Thompson, 47

They would like to pay no taxes, have no troops, and be the greatest nation in the world – all pure fantasy.

– Thompson, 141

You can keep an Italian population down only by holy fear.

– Johnston, 228

Ah! Beautiful women, well-made men, and — they understand the art of being happy.

— Table Talk, 144

JESUS

Jesus should have performed his miracles not in remote parts of Syria . . . but in a city like Rome, in front of the whole population.

— Bertrand, I, 84

The greatest republican was Jesus Christ.

— Bertaut, 151

JEWS

The Hebrews knew the true God a thousand years before other men.

— *Correspondance de Napoléon,*
"Affaires religieuses," XXIX, 568

The Jews are a vile people, cowardly and cruel.

— Gourgaud, II, 270

. . . the most despicable race in the world.

— Thompson, 213

JUDGMENT

A good idea is not always combined with a good judgment, but a good judgment always presupposes a combination of good ideas.

— Chaptal, 324

JUSTICE

Without justice there are only factions — of oppressors and of victims.

> — *Correspondance de Napoléon,*
> No. 4447, VI, 48

There is no middle ground; it is either due process or arbitrariness.

> — Damas Hinard, I, 485

JUVENILE DELINQUENT

The crimes of children are often the fruit of the bad training they received from their parents.

> — Bertaut, 38

K
KINGSHIP to KORAN

KINGSHIP

Kingship is an actor's part.

— Damas Hinard, I, 8

The love that kings inspire should be virile — partly an apprehensive respect, and partly a thirst for reputation.

— Thompson, 174-5

When a king is said to be a good fellow, his reign is a failure.

— Thompson, 175

Good nature is an affectation which a sovereign ought to avoid. What does he want? Is it to remind those who surround him that he is a man like any one? What nonsense! So soon as a man is a king he is apart from all.

— Rémusat, 134-5

A truly great man knows how to be everything by turns and according to circumstances — a master or an equal, a king or a citizen.

— Rémusat, 568

KORAN

The Koran is not just religious; it is civil and political. The Bible only preaches morals.

— Bertrand, I, 121

L
LAW to LUXURY

LAW

Laws, explicit in theory, are often chaotic in application.

— Bertaut, 122

A bad law applied is more useful than a good law reviewed.

— Bertaut, 146

Without force, law is of no avail.

— Thompson, 34

The greater part of society is not evil, for if the large majority wished to be criminals and defy the law, who would have the power to control them?

— Las Cases, I, 271

LAWYERS

Reviewers corrupt the law; lawyers kill it.

— Bertaut, 137

LIBERTY

Liberty is needed by a small and privileged class, who are gifted by nature with abilities greater than those of the bulk of mankind. It can therefore be restricted with impunity. Equality, on the other hand, delights the multitude.

— Rémusat, 506

LIES

A lie is good for nothing since it only deceives for a while.

— Bertaut, 27

He lies too much. One may very well lie sometimes, but always is too much.

— Fisher, 211

LIFE

Life is a flimsy dream, soon to be over.

— *Correspondence of Napoléon with Joseph,* No. 4, I, 5

There are three modes of life: the voluptuous, the speculative, and the active. The first leads only to vice. The enlightened man unites the second and third.

— Bertrand, I, 297

Life means suffering.

— Hortense, II, 357

LORD'S PRAYER

Do you wish to find out the really sublime? Repeat the Lord's Prayer.

— *Table Talk,* 14

LOVE

Love is a foolishness made for two.

— Bertaut, 60

Ivy will cling to the first met tree; that, in a few words,

is the whole history of love.

— Johnston, 6

What is love? The realization of his weakness that sooner or later pervades the solitary man, a sense both of his weakness and of his immortality — the soul finds support, is doubled, is fortified; the blessed tears of sympathy flow — there is love.

— Johnston, 6-7

For what is love? A passion which sets all the universe on one side, and on the other the beloved object.

— Rémusat, 94

In war, as in love, to triumph one must make contact.

— Bertaut, 168

The only victory over love is flight.

— *Table Talk,* 146

Love should be a pleasure, not a torment.

— Las Cases, I, 283

Love . . . is the occupation of the idle man, the distraction of the warrior, the stumbling-block of the sovereign.

— Las Cases, I, 284

Love is always the lot of idle societies.

— Bertaut, 56

Love! I don't quite know what that means in politics.

— Fisher, 211

Love is a melancholy business when all the affections of

one's heart are wrapped up in a single person.

— Carr, 141

Love does not really exist. It is an artificial sentiment born of society.

— Bertrand, II, 218

LUXURY

The luxuries of the rich give the necessities to the poor.

— Bertaut, 135

MAN

What a miserable thing is man! The smallest fibre in his body, assailed by disease, is sufficient to derange his whole system. On the other hand, in spite of all the maladies to which he is subject, it is sometimes necessary to employ the executioner to put an end to him.

— *Table Talk,* 76-7

To do everything one can is human; to do everything one would like to do is god-like.

— Bertaut, 36

Men only consider their needs, never their abilities.

— Martel, III, 6

The majority of men are weak, inconstant because of their weakness, seeking gain where possible, and . . . deserving to be pitied more than hated.

— Martel IV, 497

Men have their virtues and their vices, their heroism and their perversity. Men are neither generally good nor generally evil, but they possess and exercise all that is good and evil here on earth.

— Bertaut, 33

We are, after all, nothing but big babies.

— Rosebery, 104

Men in general are exacting, conceited, and frequently wrong.

— Las Cases, 171

The world is old, but mankind is young.

— Bertrand, I, 64

When we speak ill of men, we make an exception in our own favor.

— Hortense, II, 343

A man is only a man. He needs some spark to act. What is the fire that makes the kettle boil?

— Bertrand, I, 225

MARRIAGE

A mutual exchange of souls, of perspiration.

— Herold, 21

Marriage is, without question, the state of social perfection.

— Bertaut, 56

Marriage should not be permitted to individuals who have not known each other for at least six months.

— Damas Hinard, II, 105

Marriage is not always, as is supposed, the conclusion of love.

— Damas Hinard, I, 351

The woman owes obedience to her husband . . . The angel declared it to Adam and Eve. In the marriage ceremony it was said in Latin, so the woman understood nothing.

— Johnston, 151

No marriage is complete and real without children.

— Johnston, 477

MEDICINE

The art of healing is only that of lulling and calming the imagination. That is why the ancients decked themselves out in striking and imposing vestments. You [modern doctors] have abandoned the costume — that's a mistake.

— Antommarchi, I, 366

Take a dose of medicine once and in all probability you will be obliged to take an additional hundred afterwards.

— O'Meara, II, 137

Water, air, and cleanliness are my favorite medicines.

— Ludwig, 546

The [medical] laboratory has its heroes as does the battlefield, and what a difference in the results!

— Antommarchi, I, 261

MEMORY

The head without memory is a fortress without a garrison.

— Bertaut, 37

Men usually exercise their memory more than their judgment.

— Bertaut, 37

MILITARY SCIENCE

Military science consists in calculating all the chances accurately in the first place, and then in giving accident exactly, almost mathematically, its place in one's calculations. It is upon this point that one must not deceive one's self, and that a decimal more or less may change all.

— Rémusat, 135

MIRACLES

Miracles are a bad proof of the divinity of Christ.
— Bertrand, I, 182

God does not need any miracles. It would be good to believe in God as we believe in the sun. Nobody doubts of its existence.

— Bertrand, I, 182

MISFORTUNE

Misfortune is the midwife of genius.
— Bertaut, 42

Men will accept misfortune if insult be not added.
— Johnston, 268

Misfortune has its good side; it teaches us truths.
Ludwig, 639

Misfortunes come soon enough without going to look for them.

— St. Denis, 245

MODERATION

Moderation is the basis of morality and man's most important virtue.

— Damas Hinard, 103

MOHAMMED

Mohammed is the successor of Jesus Christ and Moses. He came to put down idolatry and to announce the cult of one God.

— Bertrand, I, 225

The existence of Mohammed is as uncertain as that of Jesus.

— Bertrand, I, 183

MONARCHY

It is the only form of government suitable to France.

— Caulaincourt, I, 315

MONEY

It is with money that one holds men who have money.

— Damas Hinard, I, 85

Money means everything.

— Bertrand, I, 63

MONKS

Monkish humiliation is destructive of all virtue, all energy, all management.

— Las Cases, 202

MONUMENTS

Only the dead are entitled to public monuments.

— Caulaincourt, II, 131

The primary idea that the word "monument" conveys is

of a thing indestructible, thus the pyramids — constructed of masses of stone of grandiose size — these are monuments!

— Damas Hinard, II, 323

MORALITY

There are moral laws as inflexible and imperious as the physical ones.

— Montholon, III, 186

In a country with any morals, everyone is at home by ten in the evening.

— Masson, 11

MOTIVATION

One does not fight for rights, but for interests.

— Bertrand, I, 110

There are two levers for moving men — self-interest and fear.

— Bourrienne, I, 316

MOURNING

No matter how natural your sorrow, it should have some limit.

— Hortense, II, 356

MUSIC

Of all the *beaux-arts,* music has the greatest influence on the passions and is the one the legislator most should encourage.

— Bertaut, 89

A piece of moral music from the pen of a master unfailingly touches our feelings and has much more influence than a good essay on morals, which convinces the reason without altering our habits.

— *Correspondance de Napoléon,*
No. 2042, III, 265-6

NAVAL TACTICS

On the seas nothing is genius or inspiration; everything there is positive and empiric. The admiral needs only one science, that of navigation ... An admiral has to divine nothing; he knows where the enemy is, and he knows its strength.

— Bertaut, 188

NECESSITY

There is nothing that people cannot manage to justify by necessity, especially when they constitute themselves judges of that necessity.

— Hutt, 43

NEGOTIATIONS

(Reported) "He said it was easy to know when a government wished for peace by observing the character of the person sent to treat for it."

— Meynell, 41

NEWS

It is always more interesting to give an account of a new ill than a new good.

— *Correspondance de Napoléon,*
No. 3753, V, 267

NEWSPAPERS

Four hostile newspapers are more to be feared than a thousand bayonets.

— Heinl, 236

Newspapers are influenced by party principles; what one praises the other will abuse; and so vice versa. They who live in the metropolis where they are published can judge of passing events and transactions for themselves; but persons living at a distance from the capital, and particularly foreigners, must be at a loss to determine upon the real state of things, and the characters of public men.

— Warden, 133-4

Generally speaking, our newspapers are always ready to seize on anything likely to disturb public tranquility.

— Loyd, 135

NOVELS

Books for chambermaids.

— Montholon, II, 78

NUNS

Convents attack the population at its roots. One cannot calculate the loss for the state caused by 10,000 cloistered females.

— Damas Hinard, I, 326

There is nothing too bad to expect from ill-behaved spinsters.

— Thompson, 103

OLIGARCHY

A worse, a more despotic or unforgiving government than an oligarchy never existed. Offend them once, you are never pardoned, and no treatment can be too cruel for you when in their power.

— O'Meara, II, 117

OPERA

The opera is the very soul of Paris, as Paris is the soul of France.

— Damas Hinard, 71

OPINION

It is bad manners to mix opinions with facts. One must first recount, then give one's opinions.

— Bertrand, II, 231

OPPRESSION

Next to the crime of oppressing the people, the worst crime is to accept oppression.

— Carr, 41

ORATORS

They are men of most mediocre political talents. Their strength lies in vagueness.

— Montholon, III, 188

OSTENTATION

A newly-born government must dazzle and astonish. When it ceases to do that it falls.

— Bourrienne, I, 315

Be economical and even parsimonious at home; be magnificent in public.

— Méneval, II, 414

One must have noisy celebrations for the populace. Fools love noise, and the masses are fools.

— Bertaut, 25

PARENTS to PUNISHMENT

PARENTS

When they get old they can never realize that children grow up and sometimes could actually teach them a lesson.

— Hortense, II, 336

PARLIAMENT

Parliament is a fine institution and an honor to England. It is the only thing that will survive.

— Bertrand, I, 63

PATIENCE

If you wish to study man, learn how far patience can go.

— Las Cases, II, 70

Victory belongs to the most persevering.

— *Table Talk,* 19

Impatience is a great obstacle to success. He who is determined to precipitate events does not gain anything, or else gathers green fruit which never ripens.

— Bertaut, 21

PATRIOTISM

It cannot be roused by verses and odes: it needs facts — plain facts.

— Carr, 309

To compare the days of Sparta and Rome with modern

times, I would say here reigns love, there reigned love of country.

— Masson, 14

Love of country is the first quality of civilized man.

— Correspondance de Napoléon,
No. 18962, XXIV, 72

People who have abandoned themselves to pleasure lose the ability to even conceive the existence of a patriot.

— Masson, 14

PEACE

Peace is a diagonal between two forces; it is a capitulation between the forces that fight. If one is annihilated, there is really no peace.

— Bertrand, I, 264

It is not by crying "Peace!" that one obtains it.

— Correspondance de Napoléon,
9561, XI, 574

PENAL LAWS

Penal laws should read as though engraved on tables of marble, and should be as concise as the Decalogue.

— Johnston, 129

PEOPLE

The populace is a tiger when it is unmuzzled.

— Damas Hinard, II, 281

PHILOSOPHER

A good philosopher makes a bad citizen.

— Bertaut, 80

POETRY

It's a hollow science.

— Méneval, I, 127

Verse is only the embroidery of the fabric of drama.

— Bertaut, 108

Not even the fictions of the burning of Troy, though heightened by all the powers of poetry, could have equalled the reality of the destruction of Moscow.

— *Table Talk*, 35

POLAND

Poland exists only in the imagination of those who wish to make it their pretext for creating dreams.

— *Correspondance de Napoléon*,
No. 16180, XX, 180

The Poles . . . are a trivial people.

— Caulaincourt, I, 295

POLICE

The art of the police is in punishing infrequently and severely.

— *Correspondance de Napoléon*,
No. 8922, X, 674

POLITICAL FACTIONS

Men of mark look from above and have no party ties; one who belongs to a party is a slave.

— Ludwig, 591

Factions are not to be put down so long as any fear of them is shown, and every attempt to conciliate them looks like fear.

— Rémusat, 166

Since one has to take sides, one might as well join the side which is winning; the side which destroys, loots, and burns. Considering the alternate course, it is better to eat than to be eaten.

— Iung, I, 468

POLITICAL HATRED

It is like a pair of spectacles: one sees everybody, every opinion, or every sentiment only through the glass of one's passions. Hence, nothing is bad or good of itself, but simply according to the party to which one belongs.

— Rémusat, 83

POLITICAL SCIENCE

For all our pride, our thousand and one pamphlets, and our blustering speeches, we are extremely ignorant of the science of political conduct.

— Carr, 86

POLITICAL VIRTUE

The term "political virtue" is nonsense.

— Bertaut, 94

POLITICS

Politics is destiny.

— Bertaut, 19

Politics is a cord that snaps if subjected to too great a strain.

— Masson, 226

In political administration problems are never simple. Never can they be reduced to the question of whether a certain measure is good or not.

— *Correspondance de Napoléon,*
No. 13283, XVI, 128

In politics, an absurdity is not an obstacle.

— Bertaut, 68

In politics, there is no heart, only head.

— Méneval, II, 228

The greatest evil in politics is to be without fixed precepts.

— Bertaut, 65

In politics, there is a wide gulf between promises and performances.

— *Table Talk,* 151

A policy may lead to a catastrophe without any real crime being committed.

— Johnston, 256

Government policy is only common sense applied to great things.

— Gautier, *Staël,* 403

POPE

One should render unto God that which is God's — but the pope is not God.

> — *Correspondance de Napoléon,*
> No. 17478, XXI, 566

Treat the pope as though he had 200,000 men.

> — Johnston, 188

There are probably popes in Hell, as well as parsons.

> — Thompson, 231

POPULARITY

It takes time to make one's self liked.

> — Rémusat, 95

POWER

Power is never ridiculous.

> — Fisher, 209

In this world there are only two alternatives: command or obey.

> — Caulaincourt, I, 298

There are only two powers in the world: the sword and the spirit . . . meaning civil and religious institutions . . . In the end, the sword will always be conquered by the spirit.

> — Martel, III, 7

PRIDE

Pride never listens to the voice of reason, nature, or religion.

> — *Table Talk,* 150

PRISON

The contagion of crime is like that of plague. Criminals collected together corrupt each other; they are worse than ever, when at the termination of their punishment they re-enter society.

— Table Talk, 100

PRISONERS OF WAR

Prisoners of war do not belong to the power for which they fought. They are entirely under the protection of honor, the generosity, of the nation which has disarmed them.

— Bertaut, 173

PROBABILITY

Everything is probability in life; there is no use worrying.

— Bertrand, I, 274

PROCRASTINATION

The great majority of men attend to what is necessary only when they feel a need for it — the precise time when it is too late.

— Herold, 5

PROMISES

The best way to keep your word is never to give it.

— Bertaut, 49

PROPAGANDA

The way to be believed is to make the truth incredible.

— Bertaut, 41

The publication of false news is a small means of producing incalculable effects on men whose calculations are not the result of cool heads and who each carries with him the alarms and prejudices of his clique.

— Bertaut, 23

The men who have changed the world ... never succeeded by winning over the powerful, but always by stirring the masses. The first method is a resort to intrigue and only brings limited results. The latter is the course of genius and changes the face of the world.

— Las Cases, I, 529

PROPERTY

Property is the fundamental basis of all political associations.

— Damas Hinard, I, 429

The lawgiver must arrange his political situation so that even the poorest people own something.

— Martel, I, 26

Modern nations care only about property.

— Gautier, *Dix Années,* 141

Six feet of earth is enough for a man.

— Caulaincourt, II, 130

PROPRIETY

In even the smallest things every man should stick to his own business.

— Rémusat, 551

PRUSSIA

Prussia was hatched from a cannon ball.

— Heinl, 188

PUBLIC OPINION

Public opinion is an invisible, mysterious, irresistible power. Nothing is more mobile, nothing more vague, nothing stronger. Capricious though it is, nevertheless, it is truthful, reasonable, and just much more often than one would think.

— Las Cases, I, 252

Public opinion . . . is so eager for news and for lies . . . that the more one deceives it the more easily one is believed.

— Mollien, I, 260

It must be guided without the people being aware of it.

— *Correspondance de Napoléon,*
No. 8001, IX, 644

Morale and public opinion comprise the better part of reality.

— Heinl, 196

Public opinion is the thermometer that a sovereign must consult unceasingly.

— Bertaut, 69

World opinion is made by either France or England.

— Carr, 305

PUNISHMENT

To robbers and galley slaves, physical restrictions are imposed — to enlightened people, moral ones.

— O'Meara, II, 139

RACISM

It is obvious that those who wanted liberty for the blacks wished to enslave the whites.

— Bertaut, 147

If I were black, I would be for the blacks; being white, I am for the whites.

— Herold, 5

RELIGION

Religion is a sort of inoculation or vaccine which, while satisfying our sense of the supernatural, guarantees us from the charlatans and the magicians.

— Johnston, 227

Man loves the supernatural. He meets deception halfway.

— Johnston, 482

I do not see in religion the mystery of the incarnation but the mystery of the social order. It associates with heaven an idea of equality that keeps the rich man from being massacred by the poor.

— Roederer, 18

No society can exist without morality; there is no good morality without religion. It is only religion that gives a state a firm and lasting foundation. A society without religion is like a vessel without a compass: a vessel in that condition can neither keep to its course nor hope to reach port.

— Damas Hinard, II, 389-90

A little religion is good, too much is bad.

— Bertrand, I, 285

One God, all powerful, creator and master of all is the simplest and most reasonable idea.

— Bertrand, I, 225

The idea of God is very useful — to maintain good order, to keep men in the path of virtue and to keep them from crime.

— Bertrand, I, 182

A man must be a good deal of a fool if he thinks there is nothing superior to his own ideas.

— Carr, 231

Society cannot exist without inequality of fortunes, and inequality of fortunes cannot exist without religion. When a man is dying of hunger beside another who has engorged himself, it is impossible for him to accept that difference unless there is an authority that tells him to.

— Roederer, 18

Were I obliged to have a religion, I would worship the sun — the source of all life — the real god of the earth.

— Rosebery, 188

The most horrible of all tyrannies is that which forces . . . a nation to embrace a religion against their beliefs.

— *Moniteur,* October 15, 1803

A just and wise toleration in religion is a benefit to governments. A religion is only a law which directs the conscience. So long as it undertakes to follow the impulse of nature in all that is good and social, when it purifies morals and rejects everything which can injure the propagation of the human race, order, liberty, it ought to be adopted, protected, and supported.

— St. Denis, 242

Without religion, we walk continually in darkness, and the Catholic religion is the only one that gives man certain knowledge of his origin and final purpose.

— Damas Hinard, I, 207

The three religions that have spread the knowledge of an immortal God, uncreated, master and creator of man, all sprang from Arabia. Moses, Jesus Christ, and Mohammed were Arabs.

— *Correspondance de Napoléon,*
"Affaires religieuses," XXIX, 571

One crushes a religious nation; one does not divide it.

— Bertaut, 157

Information and history . . . are the great enemies of true religion, so disfigured by human imperfections.

— Las Cases, II, 194

The essential laws of the church are, "Thou shalt not hurt society," "Thou shalt do no ill to thy neighbor," and "Thou shalt not misuse thy liberty."

— Bertaut, 22

REPRESENTATIVE GOVERNMENT

An absolute power has no need to lie; it is silent. Representative government, being obliged to speak, dissembles and lies shamelessly.

— Las Cases, I, 706

When a nation is at war, the presence of a deliberative body is injurious and often fatal.

— Heinl, 64

Nothing can be worse for a nation than the power of expressing its will without being listened to.

— Rémusat, 617

REPUBLIC

You cannot make republics from old monarchies.

— Bertaut, 75

RETREAT

In a retreat, besides the honor of the army, a commander often loses more men than in two battles.

— Lanza, 22

REVOLUTION

A revolution is an opinion that finds bayonets.

— Bertaut, 82

Young people accomplish the revolutions that old men prepared.

— Bertaut, 83

Once the first gun is fired, there are no more explanations; passions rise and men who cannot agree kill each other.

— Caulaincourt, I, 310

General rule: Never a social revolution without terror.

— Las Cases, II, 300

The only use of revolutionary theories is to destroy counterrevolutionary theories.

— Bertrand, I, 129

A revolution is one of the greatest evils heaven has visited upon earth: the scourge of the generation which produces it.

— Carr, 366

All the benefits it procures cannot compensate for the misery with which it embitters the lives of the participants.

— Carr, 366

A revolution is merely a revolt which success and time have legitimized.

— Montholon, I, 211

In times of revolution, precedents become law.

— Thompson, 14

In revolutions there are only two kinds of people — those who make them and those who profit from them.

— Bertaut, 82

In revolutions everything is forgotten. The benefits you confer today, are forgotten tomorrow. The side once changed, gratitude, friendship, parentage, every tie vanishes, and all sought for is self-interest.

— O'Meara, I, 51

As soon as they begin a revolt, the people cease to be right.

— Lecestre, II, 70

When the mob gains the day, it ceases to be any longer

the mob. It is then called the nation. If it does not, why then some are executed, and they are called *canaille,* rebels, robbers, and so forth.

— O'Meara, I, 263

REWARDS

To give reasonably is to honor; to give in excess is to corrupt.

— Bertaut, 51

RIOTS

You don't express the will of the people by bribing a handful of armed men to raise a riot.

— Thompson, 87

I fear insurrections caused by a lack of bread. I would be less afraid of a battle against 200,000 men.

— Chaptal, 285

If you treat the mob with kindness, these creatures fancy themselves invulnerable; if you hang a few, they get tired of the game, and become as submissive and humble as they ought to be.

— *Correspondence of Napoléon
with Joseph,* No. 483, II, 15

The people never chafe themselves against naked bayonets.

— Heinl, 31

It is the worst possible policy to fire powder only in the beginning. For the populace after the first discharge, hearing a great noise, are a little frightened, but looking around them, and seeing nobody killed or wounded, pluck up their spirits, begin immediately to despise you, become doubly outrageous, and rush on without fear, and it is necessary to kill ten times the number that would have been done had ball been used at first.

$-$ O'Meara, I, 270-1

With a rabble, everything depends upon the first impression made upon them.

$-$ O'Meara, I, 271

ROME

The world can totally change. Rome never changes, and that is really something.

$-$ Bertrand, II, 346

ROUSSEAU

The principles of Rousseau are in general ridiculous, but some of them are useful.

$-$ Bertrand, I, 270

RULING

One rules men better by their vices than by their virtues.

$-$ Bertaut, 23

In affairs of state one must never retreat, never retrace one's steps, never admit an error $-$ that brings disrepute.

$-$ Ségur, 132

The art of appointing men is not nearly so difficult as the art of allowing those appointed to attain their full worth.

$-$ Mollien, I, 314

So long as a prince holds his tongue, his power is incalculable; he should never talk, unless he knows he is the ablest man in the room.

> — Thompson, 121

No people are bad under a good government.

> — Thiébault, II, 16

A new government must dazzle and amaze; the moment it ceases to do so, it falls.

> — Bertaut, 199

One of the most important qualities in a monarch should be indulgence. I am prepared to forgive all those who only betrayed *me*.

> — Hortense, II, 202

If a ruler does good, people will know it after his death and then praise him, but in order to be obeyed while he is alive he must seem cruel in order to be feared.

> — Hortense, II, 376

It is quite difficult to govern when one wants to do it conscientiously.

> — Bertaut, 66

A man who is not the strongest should be the most politic.

> — Caulaincourt, I, 59

Men are like ciphers who acquire value only by their position.

> — Damas Hinard, I, 574

In the last analysis, one must be a soldier to rule.

> — Bertaut, 90

Good and upstanding people must be persuaded by gentle means — the rabble must be moved by terror.

— Lecestre, II, 133

You will not lead the populace by coaxing it . . . Energy is what is wanted.

— Loyd, 203-4

RUSSIA

Europe should think of only one enemy, and that enemy is the Russian colossus.

— Caulaincourt, I, 278

Russia is the power that marches the most surely, and with the greatest strides, towards universal dominion.

— Rosebery, 220

[If] once mistress of Constantinople, Russia gets all the commerce of the Mediterranean, becomes a great naval power, and God knows what may happen.

— O'Meara, II, 31

Above all the other powers, Russia is the most to be feared.

— O'Meara, II, 31

Russia is a dreadful power and one that seems to consider it a duty to conquer Europe.

— Bertrand, I, 208

The Russians are a nation of barbarians and . . . their strength lies in their cunning.

— Lecestre, I, 51

Barbarians, who . . . have no country, and to whom every country is better than the one which gave them birth.

— O'Meara, I, 235

Russia . . . a country away at the back of beyond.

— Caulaincourt, I, 8

We must . . . cure the Russians of their curiosity about what goes on in Germany.

— Caulaincourt, I, 52

[War between] Russia and America? Impossible.

— O'Meara, I, 321

Distance makes her harmless.

— *Correspondance de Napoléon,*
No. 892, VII, 76

SABBATH to SWITZERLAND

SABBATH

For those who are at their ease, it may be very right and proper to discontinue working on the seventh day, but to oblige a poor man who has a large family, without a meal to give them, to leave off laboring to procure them victuals, is the height of barbarity.

— O'Meara, II, 202

SATIRE

There are some things too serious to joke about.

— Bertrand, I, 30

SECRETS

If you wish to keep your private affairs secret, keep your servants well paid.

— Bertaut, 68

SEX

La vie intime is the guarantee of a good household. It assures the credit of the wife and the dependence of the husband. It maintains intimacy and morals.

— Bertaut, 60

SHAKESPEARE

It is impossible to finish reading one of his plays; they are pitiful.

— Damas Hinard, I, 438

SLAVERY

In Roman times, the slave could be freed, but he retained a dishonest and base character, never being considered as being like a citizen born free. Colonial slavery, established on the difference of color, is much more rigid and debasing.

— Damas Hinard, I, 441

SMOKING

. . . good for nothing but to enliven idlers.

— Constant, II, 11

SOCIAL PROTOCOL

It is a device of fools to raise themselves to the level of people of intellect; a sort of social gag, which obstructs the strong mind and only serves the weak. It may be all very well for women: they have not much to do in this life.

— Rémusat, 102

SOCIETY

There is always between a man and woman a certain gallantry that does not exist between man and man.

— Bertrand, II, 221

SOLDIERS

In order to have good soldiers, a nation must always be at war.

— O'Meara, I, 108

When defending itself against another country, a nation never lacks men, but too often, soldiers.

— Heinl, 180

A soldier is only a machine to obey orders.

— *Table Talk,* 6

Of all men, the soldier is the most responsive to rewards.

— Bertaut, 180

The soldier follows the fortune and misfortune of his general; his honor is his religion.

— *Correspondance de Napoléon,*
No. 21557, XXVII, 492

Soldiers generally win battles; generals get credit for them.

— Heinl, 338

Poverty, privation and misery are the true school of a soldier.

— Bertaut, 176

The first qualities of a soldier are constancy and discipline: valor is only secondary.

— *Correspondance de Napoléon,*
No. 4450, VI, 49-50

The distinctive mark of the soldier is that all his desires are despotic; that of the civilian is that he submits everything to discussion, to truth, to reason.

— Johnston, 159

SOUL

If one has bad morals he must learn to care for his soul as one cares for an arm or a leg.

— Damas Hinard, I, 40

When we are dead . . . we are altogether dead.

— Rosebery, 188

SPANISH

The Spanish people are vile and cowardly — on a par with the Arabs.

— Lecestre, I, 241

The Spanish peasantry have even less share in the civilization of Europe than the Russians.

— Caulaincourt, I, 307

The Spaniards have shown themselves opinionated and cruel, but not brave.

— Bertrand, II, 216

SPELLING

A man occupied with public or other important business cannot, and need not, attend to spelling.

— Prochnow, 314

SPIES

Don't trust spies. They are more trouble than they are worth.

— Thompson, 121

STATESMAN

The heart of a statesman must be in his head.

— Las Cases, II, 611

[He] approaches to being a statesman – he lies very well.

— Rémusat, 4

Is a great statesman made for feeling? Is he not a completely eccentric personage, who stands always alone, on his own side, with the world on the other?

— Rémusat, 136

The glass through which [the statesman] looks is that of his policy; his sole concern ought to be that it should neither magnify nor diminish. And, while he observes objects with attention, he must also be careful to hold the reins equally; for the chariot which he drives is often drawn by ill-matched horses.

— Rémusat, 136

STOCK MARKET

All that those so-called buyers and sellers do is take bets with one another on the prevailing market prices on such and such a date. As a consequence, every one of them, in order to win his bet, . . . invents facts, comments on facts, disfugures facts.

— Mollien, I, 259

STUPIDITY

Rascality has limits, stupidity has not.

— Prochnow, 319

No one is so stupid as not to be good for something.

— Roederer, 237

SUCCESS

A nation, like history itself, rarely takes account of anything but success.

— Caulaincourt, I, 360

SUICIDE

Does a man have the right to kill himself? Yes, if his death harms no other person and if life is ill for him.

— *Correspondance de Napoléon,*
"Reflexions sur le suicide,"
XXXI, 579

A man shows more real courage in supporting and resisting the calamities and misfortunes which befall him, than by making away with himself. That is the action of a losing gamester, or a ruined spendthrift, and is a want of courage, instead of a proof of it.

— O'Meara, I, 33

It certainly originates in that species of fear which we denominate cowardice. For what claim can that man have to courage who trembles at the frowns of fortune?

— Warden, 58

Suicide? . . . those who wish me well would not be benefited, and it would give pleasure to those who wish me ill.

— Campbell, 172

One commits suicide to escape disgrace, not to escape misfortune.

— Hortense, II, 106

SWITZERLAND

There are no people more impudent or more demanding than the Swiss. Their country is about as big as a man's hand, and they have the most extraordinary pretensions.

— Bertrand, I, 93

TAXES

The income tax is a good tax, for everyone grumbles at it, which shows that everyone pays it.

— Rosebery, 36

THEOLOGY

It is with water and not with oil that one calms theological disputes.

— Damas Hinard, II, 342-3

Theology is a sewer of every kind of superstition and error.

— Masson, 63

TIME

Fools talk of the past, wise men of the present, and madmen of the future.

— Bertaut, 41

Occupation is the scythe of time.

— *Table Talk,* 60

TITLES

Distinctions of this kind . . . are very generally coveted, because it is only human nature to want to leave one's children some memorial of the reputation one has enjoyed.

— Thompson, 200

. . . titles cost nothing.

— Johnston, 229-30

TRADE

Trade is an honorable pursuit, if conducted with prudence and economy. . . . A merchant must not gain his fortune as one gains a battle; he must make small and continual profits.

— Miot de Melito, 573

To manufacture is not enough; it is necessary to know where and how to sell, and not to make ten yards of stuff where there is only sale for four.

— Miot de Melito, 573

Free commerce . . . aids all classes, stirs all imaginations, moves all people; it is identical with equality.

— Damas Hinard, I, 265-6

TRUTH

Only the truth wounds.

— O'Meara, I, 265

UNIFORMS to UTILITY

UNIFORMS

The strength [of troops] is not in the color of their clothing as the strength of Samson was in his hair.

— Damas Hinard, II, 543

A soldier must learn to love his profession, must look to it to satisfy all his tastes and his sense of honor. That is why handsome uniforms are useful.

— Heinl, 333

UNITED STATES OF AMERICA

This accession of territory [Louisiana] fixes forever the power of the United States, and . . . gives England a maritime rival that will sooner or later humble her.

— Damas Hinard, II, 77

Everything progresses without noticeable use of force . . . This is because the people's wishes and interests are, in fact, the governing power. Let that same government oppose their will and interests and you will see how quickly disturbance, disagreement, anxiety, confusion, and above all increased crime, will follow.

— Las Cases, II, 513

The English will end by subscribing to all that the Americans desire, and the American government, placed in the hands of able statesmen, will gain increased strength. It will profit by the opportunity to make the nation give it the means of organizing and maintaining a larger army, . . . and in the future that country will be England's most powerful adversary. Before thirty years have passed, it will make her tremble.

— Caulaincourt, I, 371-2

UNITY OF COMMAND

One bad general is better than two good ones.

— Thompson, 26

UNKNOWN

In the imagination as in mathematics, the value of the unknown is incalculable.

— Las Cases, II, 608

UTILITY

Here is what most men demand of you: Be useful to me.

— Bertrand, II, 245

It is not the *utility* of an act which is to be considered, it is its justice; for by the former principle, every species of crime may be apparently justified as being useful, and therefore necessary.

— O'Meara, II, 140

VANITY to VICTORY

VANITY

One must be very vain to dress simply.

— Hortense, II, 23

VICTORY

There are no enemies after a victory, but only men.

— Ségur, 83

Remember the words of a Roman Emperor: "A dead enemy always smells sweet."

— Caulaincourt, I, 77

WATERLOO to WOMEN

WATERLOO

The plan of the battle will not in the eyes of the historian reflect any credit on Lord Wellington as a general. . . . The glory of such a victory is a great thing; but in the eye of the historian, his military reputation will gain nothing by it.

— O'Meara, I, 284-6

WAR

What is war? A barbarous profession whose art consists in being stronger than the enemy at a given moment.

— Ségur, 63

War is a lottery in which nations should risk only small stakes.

— Bertaut, 77

The mistakes of our enemies often serve them to better purpose than the talents of their generals and lead us into even greater errors ourselves.

— Caulaincourt, I, 377

In war, a great disaster always indicates a great culprit.

— Bertaut, 177

Inevitable wars are always just.

— Bertaut, 164

Everything is moral in war.

— Thompson, 254

Victories are glamorous up to the age of thirty and the horrors of war may be glossed over, but after that . . . .

— Ségur, 98

To the cannon, all men are equal.

— Bertrand, II, 344

In war, one does not need so much cunning. The simplest thing is the best.

— Bertrand, II, 341

There is no such thing as intellect in war, especially not at the speed with which we make war today.

— Bertrand, I, 4

In war, the side which stays behind its fortified lines is always defeated.

— Martel, I, 169

The art of war is like everything else that is beautiful and simple — the simplest moves are the best.

— Gourgaud, II, 460

In warfare one sees one's own deficiencies, but not those of the enemy.

— Johnston, 310

If the art of war be only the art of risking nothing, glory would become the prey of mediocrities.

— Fain, II, 26

All offensive war is a war of invasion.

— Damas Hinard, I, 549

You must not fight too often with one enemy, or you

will teach him all your art of war.

— Heinl, 102

When bayonets deliberate, power escapes from the hands of the government.

— Heinl, 31

Blood-letting is one of the remedies in political medicine.

— Rémusat, 138

War should be made methodically, for it should have a definite object.

— Lanza, 8

If you make war, wage it with energy and severity; it is the only means of making it shorter, and consequently less deplorable for mankind.

— *Correspondance de Napoléon,*
No. 4478, VI, 72-3

Nothing is absolute in war.

— Lanza, 55

War will become an anachronism. . . . Victories will be won some day without cannon and bayonets.

— Bertaut, 182-3

War is a business of good sense, perseverance, and resolution.

— Bertrand, II, 347

WELFARE

To revive a nation, it is much simpler to deal with its

inhabitants a thousand at a time than to pursue the romantic ideal of individual welfare.

— Correspondance de Napoléon,
No. 582, I, 412

WELLINGTON

. . . a man of little genius, without generosity, and without greatness of soul.

— O'Meara, II, 132

(Reported) "Of the abilities of the Duke of Wellington, he remarked that it would one day be of bad consequence to the English nation, who would expect more from their army than they had capacity for, when not guided by superior knowledge."

— Maynell, 45

WILL

The greater one is, the less will he must have. He depends on events and circumstances.

— Herold, 43

WISDOM

Learn to listen, and remember that silence is often as effective as a display of knowledge.

— Thompson, 120

To know when to stop is sometimes the best proof of understanding.

— Table Talk, 37

WOMEN

Two things are very becoming to women – rouge and tears.

– Rémusat, 127

Conversation is never so lively or so witty as when ladies take part in it.

– O'Meara, II, 109

Equality for women? That is madness. Women are our property; we are not theirs. They give us children . . . and belong to us as the fruit-bearing tree belongs to the gardener.

– Damas Hinard, I, 477-8

What we ask of education is not that girls should think, but that they should believe. The weakness of women's brains, the instability of their ideas, the place they will fill in society, their need for perpetual resignation, and for an easy and generous type of charity – all this can only be met by religion.

– Thompson, 195

A public education does not suit them, for the reason that they are not called on to live in public; for them habit is everything, and marriage is the goal.

– Johnston, 226

Nothing announces rank, education, and good breeding in women . . . more than the evenness of their disposition and the desire to please.

– *Table Talk,* 71

Women should not be looked upon as equals of men. They are, in actuality, only machines for making babies.

– Gourgaud, I, 390

Women, when they are bad, are worse than men, and more ready to commit crimes. The soft sex, when degraded, falls lower than the other. Women are always much better or much worse than men.

– O'Meara, II, 19

Women . . . are brave, susceptible of great excitement, and capable of committing the worst atrocities. If war came between men and women, it would be very much different from the struggles the world has seen between nobles and the people or the blacks and the whites.

– Gourgaud, I, 390-1

The man who allows himself to be ruled by his wife is neither himself, nor his wife – he is nothing.

– Bertaut, 58-9

Women are full of intrigue and should be kept at home and away from politics.

– Bertaut, 90

They should be forbidden to appear in public except in a black skirt and veil.

– Masson and Biagi, 87

One should never argue with women; in silence one must listen to their nonsense.

– Bertaut, 61

In great crises the lot of women is to soften our reverses.

– Damas Hinard, I, 476

[There is] a fundamental distinction of sex and of education [between men and women] : You are made for love, and you are taught to say *no*. We, on the contrary, glory in saying *yes*, even when we should not.

– Johnston, 478

The woman we love is always the most beautiful of her sex.

– Table Talk, 147

A woman needs six months in Paris to know what is her due and her empire.

– Correspondance de Napoléon,
No. 44, I, 61-2

A beautiful woman pleases the eye; a good woman pleases the heart – one is a jewel, the other a treasure.

– Bertaut, 58

Ah! tears! Woman's only weapon.

– Rémusat, 165

Marry a German. . . . They are the best women in the world: gentle, artless, and as fresh as roses.

– Masson, 266

Women are always pleased at being noticed, even though one criticizes them a little.

– Hortense, II, 331

After paying them the compliment of saying that they are well dressed, what else is there to talk about?

– Hortense, I, 45

Ah, these young women! They are harder to keep in order than a regiment.

– Hortense, II, 41

So long as men are dominated by passion, women can sway them.

– Masson, 207

Y
YOUTH

Only youth can have patience, because it has the future before it.

— Rémusat, 97

Youth, like the nation, clings to equality.

— Caulaincourt, I, 341

BIBLIOGRAPHY

Abbot, John S. C. *Confidential Correspondence of the Emperor Napoleon and the Empress Josephine* . . . New York: 1856

Antommarchi, Francesco, *Mémoires du docteur F. Antommarchi, ou les derniers momens de Napoléon.* Paris: 1825

Bausset, Louis Francois Joseph de. *Mémoires anecdotiques sur l'intérieur du Palais et sur Quelques événemens de l'Empire depuis 1805 jusqu'au 1er mai 1814 pour servir a l'histoire de Napoléon par L.-F.J. de Bausset.* Paris: 1829

Bertaut, Jules (ed.) *Napoléon Bonaparte; Virilités: Maximes et Pensées.* Paris: *circa* 1912

Bertrand, Henri. *Cahiers de Sainte-Hélène.* Deciphered by Paul Fleuriot de Langle. 3 vols. Paris: 1951

Bourrienne, Louis Antoine Fauvelet de. *Memoirs of Napoleon Banaparte by Louis Antoine Fauvelet de Bourrienne, His Private Secretary, to which are added an Account of the Important Events of the Hundred Days, of Napoleon's Surrender to the English, and of His Residence and Death at St. Helena, with Anecdotes and Illustrative Extracts from All the Most Authentic Sources.* Ed. by R. W. Phipps. New York: 1891

Breed, Lewis Claflin (ed) *The Opinions and Reflections of Napoleon,* Boston: 1925

Campbell, Sir Neil. *Napoleon at Fontainebleau and Elba; Being a Journal of Occurrences in 1814-1815 with Notes of Conversations by the Late Major-General Sir Neil Campbell* . . . Ed. by Archibald Neil Campbell Maclachlan. London: 1869

Caulaincourt, Armand-Augustin-Louis de. *With Napoleon in Russia; The Memoirs of General de Caulaincourt, Duke of Vicenza.* Ed. by Jean Hanoteau. Translated by George Libaire. New York: 1935 (cited as Caulaincourt I)

_____ *No Peace With Napoleon! Concluding the Memoirs of General de Caulaincourt, Duke of Vicenza.*

Ed. by Jean Hanoteau. Translated by George Libaire. New York: 1936 (cited as Caulaincourt II)

Chaptal de Chanteloup, Jean A. C. *Mes Souvenirs sur Napoléon par le Cte Chaptal, publiés par son arrière-petit-fils le Vte An. Chaptal secrétaire d'ambassade.* Paris: 1893

Constant. *Memoirs of Constant, First Valet de chambre of the Emperor on the Private Life of Napoleon, His Family and His Court.* Translated by Elizabeth Gilbert Martin. New York: 1907

Damas Hinard, (ed) *Napoléon; ses Opinions et Jugements sur les Hommes et sur les Choses; Recueilles par ordre alphabétique avec une introduction et des notes.* Paris: 1838

Fain, Francois. *Manuscrit de Mil huit cent treize, contenant le précis des événemens de cette année pour servir à l'histoire de l'Emperor Napoléon; par le Baron Fain, secrétaire du cabinet a cette époque.* Paris: 3rd Edition. 1829

Fisher, H. A. L. *Napoleon.* London: 1912

Gautier, Paul. *Madame de Staël et Napoleon.* Paris: 1903

Gourgaud, Gaspard. *Journal de Sante-Hélène: Journal inédit de 1815 à 1818.* Paris: n.d.

Heinl, Col. Robert Debs, Jr. *Dictionary of Military and Naval Quotations.* Annapolis: 1966

Herold, J. Christopher. *The Mind of Napoleon; A Selection from His Written and Spoken Words.* New York: 1955

Holtman, Robert B. *The Napoleonic Revolution.* Philadelphia and New York: 1967

Hutt, Maurice. *Great Lives Observed: Napoleon.* Englewood Cliffs: 1972

Ireland, W. H. *The Napoleon Anecdotes: Illustrating the Mental Energies of the Late Emperor of France; and the Character and Actions of His Contemporary Statesmen and Warriors.* London: 1822

Iung, Theodore. *Lucien Bonaparte et ses mémoires, 1775-1840 d'apres les papiers déposés aux archives étrangères et d'autres documents inédits.* Paris: 1882

Johnston, R. M. (ed) *The Corsican; A Diary of Napoleon's Life in His Own Words.* Boston and New York: 1930

Lanza, Conrad H. (ed) *Napoleon and Modern War; His Military Maxims.* Harrisburg, Pa: 1954

Las Cases, Emmanuel de. *Le Mémorial de Sainte-Hélène; première Edition intégrale et critique établie et annotée par Marcel Dunan de l'Institut.* Paris: 1951

Lecestre, Léon (ed) *Lettres inédites de Napoléon Ier (An VIII-1815) publiées par Léon Lecestre.* Paris: 2nd Edition. 1897

Loyd, Lady Mary (ed) *New Letters of Napoleon I Omitted from the Edition Published under the Auspices of Napoleon III.* London: 1898

Ludwig, Emil. *Napoleon,* Translated by Eden and Cedar Paul. New York: 1924

Maitland, Captain F. L. *Narrative of the Surrender of Buonaparte and of His Residence on Board H.M.S. Bellerophon; with a Detail of the Principal Events that Occured in That Ship, between the 24th of May and the 8th of August, 1815.* London: 2nd Edition. 1826

Malcolm, Sir Pulteney. *A Diary of St. Helena; The Journal of Lady Malcolm (1816, 1817) Containing the Conversations of Napoleon with Sir Pulteney Malcolm.* Ed. by Sir Arthur Wilson. London: New Edition. 1829

Marchand, L.J.N. (ed) *Précis des guerres de César, par Napoleon, écrit par M. Marchand, à l'ile Sainte-Hélène, sous la dictée de l'Empereur; suivi de plusieurs fragmens inédits.* Paris: 1836

Marquiset, Alfred. *Napoléon sténographié au conseil d'Etat, 1804-1805.* Ed. by Alfred Marquiset. Paris: 1913

Martel, Tancrède (ed) *Mémoires et Oeuvres de Napoléon, illustrés d'apres les estampes et les tableaux du temps et précédés d'une étude littéraire.* Paris: n.d.

Masson, Frédéric and Guido Biagi. (eds) *Napoléon; Manuscrits inédites, 1786-1791, publiés d'apres les originaux autographes.* Paris: 1910

Méneval, C. F. de. *Memoirs of Napoleon Bonaparte; The Court of the First Empire.* New York: 1910

Meynell, Henry. *Conversations with Napoleon at St. Helena.* London: 1911

Miot de Melito, André Francois de. *Memoirs of Count Miot de Melito; Minister, Ambassador, Councillor of State, and Member of the Institute of France, Between the Years 1788 and 1815.* Ed. by General Fleischmann. Translated by Cashel Hoey and John Lillie. New York: 1881

Mollien, Francois Nicolas. *Mémoires d'un ministre du Trésor public, 1780-1815.* Paris: 1898

Moniteur, Le (Paris)

Montholon, C. T. *Récits de la Captivité de l'Empereur a Ste. Hélène.* Paris: 1847

Napoleon I. *The Confidential Correspondence of Napoleon Bonaparte with His Brother Joseph, Sometime King of Spain.* London: 1855

——————— *Correspondance de Napoléon Ier Publiée par ordre de L'Empereur Napoléon III.* Paris: 1858-1870.

——————— *Unpublished Correspondence of Napoleon I Preserved in the War Archives.* Ed. by Ernest Picard and Louis Tuetey. Translated by Louise Seymour Houghton. New York: 1913

Noailles, Marquis de. *The Life and Memoirs of Count Molé.* London: 1890

O'Meara, Barry E. *Napoleon in Exile; or, A Voice from St. Helena. The Opinions and Reflections of Napoleon on the Most Important Events of His Life and Government, in His Own Words.* New York: 1890

Prochnow, Herbert V. and Herbert V. Prochnow, Jr. *A Treasury of Humorous Quotations.* New York: 1969

Rémusat, Paul de (ed) *Memoirs of Madame de Rémusat; 1802-1808.* Translated by Mrs. Cashel Hoey and John Lillie. New York: 1880

Roederer, Pierre Louis. *Autour de Bonaparte; Journal du Comte P.-L. Roederer, ministre et conseiller d'Etat; Notes intimes et politiques d'un familiér des Tuileries.* Paris: 1909

Rosebery, The Earl of. *Napoleon; The Last Phase.* New York and London: 1901

Ségur, Philippe Paul de. *Napoleon's Russian Campaign.* Translated by J. David Townsend. Boston: 1958

Staël, Germaine Necker de. *Dix Années d'Exil; Edition nouvelle; d'apres les manuscrits, avec une introduction, des notes et un appendice, par Paul Gautier.* Paris: 2nd Edition. 1904

St. Denis, Louis Etienne. *Napoleon; From the Tuileries to St. Helena; Personal Recollections of the Emperor's Second Mameluke and Valet, Louis Etienne St. Denis (Known as Ali).* Translated by Frank Hunter Potter. New York and London: 1922

The Table Talk and Opinions of Napoleon Buonaparte. Philadelphia: 7th Edition. 1889

Thompson, J. M. (ed) *Napoleon Self-Revealed.* Boston and New York: 1934

Warden, William. *Letters Written on Board His Majesty's Ship the Northumberland, and Saint Helena; in which the Conduct and Conversations of Napoleon Buonaparte, and His Suite, During the Voyage, and the First Months of His Residence in That Island, are Faithfully Described and Related.* London: 4th Edition. 1816